Christmas

Drink Recipes

Hannie P. Scott

www.HanniePScott.com

www.Hanniepscott.com

ISBN: 9781973540922

MY FREE GIFT TO YOU!

55

Quick

&

Easy

Recipes

hannie p. scott

To download your free gift, simply visit:

www.hanniepscott.com/freegift

TABLE OF CONTENTS

For more books by Hannie, please visit:
www.Hanniepscott.com/books

ABBREVIATIONS

oz = ounce

fl oz = fluid ounce

tsp = teaspoon

tbsp = tablespoon

ml = milliliter

c = cup

pt = pint

qt = quart

gal = gallon

L = liter

CONVERSIONS

1/2 fl oz = 3 tsp = 1 tbsp = 15 ml

1 fl oz = 2 tbsp = 1/8 c = 30 ml

2 fl oz = 4 tbsp = 1/4 c = 60 ml

4 fl oz = 8 tbsp = 1/2 c = 118 ml

8 fl oz = 16 tbsp = 1 c = 236 ml

16 fl oz = 1 pt = 1/2 qt = 2 c = 473 ml

128 fl oz = 8 pt = 4 qt = 1 gal = 3.78 L

COCKTAILS

Hot Buttered Rum

Servings: 4

What you need:

- 2 cups water
- 1/2 stick butter
- 1/4 cup packed brown sugar
- 1 tsp cinnamon
- 1/2 tsp freshly grated nutmeg
- 1/4 tsp ground cloves
- 1/8 tsp salt
- 2/3 cup dark rum

What to do:

1. In a medium saucepan over medium-high heat, bring the water, butter, brown sugar, cinnamon, nutmeg, cloves, and salt to a boil.
2. Reduce heat and simmer, stirring occasionally, for 10 minutes.
3. Remove from the heat, stir in the rum, and serve.

Holiday Sangria

Servings: 10

What you need:

- 2 bottles Pinot Grigio
- 1 cup sparkling apple cider
- 1/4 cup sugar
- 1/4 cup cranberries, cut in half
- 3/4 cup cranberries, whole
- 1 apple, cored and chopped

What to do:

1. Combine all of the ingredients in a pitcher and stir until the sugar dissolves. Refrigerate for at least 2 hours before serving.

Spiced White Chocolate Cocoa

Servings: 12

What you need:

- 16 oz good quality white chocolate, chopped
- 4 cups milk
- 4 cups heavy cream
- 1 tbsp vanilla extract
- 1/4 tsp ground nutmeg
- 3 cinnamon sticks
- Whipped cream

What to do:

1. Place the white chocolate in the bottom of your crock pot.
2. Add all the remaining ingredients except the whipped cream to the crock pot and stir.
3. Cook on low for 2 hours, stirring occasionally.
4. Ladle into mugs and top with whipped cream to serve.

Kahlua Hot Chocolate

Servings: 2

What you need:

- 2 cups whole milk
- 1/2 cup chocolate sauce
- 4 oz Kahlua
- Whipped cream
- Extra chocolate sauce for drizzling

What to do:

1. In a medium saucepan over medium heat, combine the milk and chocolate sauce. Bring to a simmer.
2. Remove from heat and stir in the Kahlua.
3. Transfer to mugs and top with whipped cream and drizzle with chocolate sauce.

Gingerbread Martini

Servings: 1

What you need:

- 1 1/2 oz vodka
- 1/2 oz brandy
- 2 oz coffee-mate gingerbread latte
- Cinnamon, as garnish

What to do:

1. Shake all of the ingredients together in a shaker and strain into a chilled martini glass.
2. Garnish with cinnamon and serve.

caramel apple sangria

Servings: 10-12

What you need:

- 1 750ml bottle of Pinot Grigio
- 1 cup caramel vodka
- 6 cups apple cider
- 2 medium apples, cored and sliced

What to do:

1. Stir the wine, vodka, and apple cider together in a large pitcher or punch bowl.
2. Add the chopped apples to the pitcher or punch bowl.
3. Serve over ice.

Andes Mint Hot Chocolate

Servings: 4-5

What you need:

- 1 bag Andes crème de menthe baking chips
- 2 cups Rumchata
- 2 cups half and half
- 2 cups milk
- Marshmallows

What to do:

1. Put all of the ingredients in your crock pot and cook on high for an hour, stirring occasionally.
2. Turn your crock pot to low or warm and serve topped with marshmallows.

Andes peppermint Hot Chocolate

Servings: 4-5

What you need:

- 1 bag Andes mint peppermint crunch baking chips
- 2 cups Rumchata
- 2 cups half and half
- 2 cups milk
- Marshmallows

What to do:

1. Put all of the ingredients in your crock pot and cook on high for an hour, stirring occasionally.
2. Turn your crock pot to low or warm and serve topped with marshmallows.

Dirty Santa

Servings: 1

What you need:

- 4 oz coffee, frozen into ice cubes
- 4 oz Bailey's Irish Cream
- 1 oz vanilla vodka

What to do:

1. Place the coffee ice cubes in a glass.
2. Pour the Bailey's and vodka in a shaker and strain over the ice.
3. Serve!

Spiced Eggnog

Makes about 1 quart

What you need:

- 1 quart store-bought eggnog
- 1/4 cup spiced rum
- 1/4 cup Kahlua
- 2 tbsp bourbon
- 1/2 tsp vanilla extract
- Ground cinnamon
- Ground cloves
- Ground nutmeg
- Brown sugar

What to do:

1. Place the eggnog, rum, Kahlua, bourbon, and vanilla in your blender and pulse for a few seconds.
2. Rim glasses with brown sugar.
3. Pour eggnog into each glass.
4. Sprinkle eggnog with cinnamon, cloves, and nutmeg.
5. Serve!

Holiday White Wine Spritzer

Servings: 20+

What you need:

- 1 liter Barefoot Moscato White Wine
- 1 liter diet sprite
- 1 liter red cream soda
- 12 oz frozen raspberries

What to do:

1. Pour the wine, sprite, and cream soda in a large pitcher or punch bowl.
2. Add the frozen raspberries and serve.

caramel Apple Hot Toddy

Servings: 8-10

What you need:

- 1 1/2 cups caramel vodka
- 1/2 gallon apple cider
- 1/2 cup bourbon
- 3 cinnamon sticks
- Whipped cream

What to do:

1. In a saucepan over medium-low heat, mix together the vodka, cider, bourbon, and cinnamon sticks until heated through.
2. Ladle into mugs and top with whipped cream before serving.

The Grinch

Servings: 1

What you need:

- 1 large scoop of lime sherbet
- 1 cup of ginger ale
- 2 oz whipped cream vodka or regular vodka
- Green decorating sugar

What to do:

1. Rim a tall glass with green decorating sugar.
2. In your blender, mix together the sherbet, ginger ale, and vodka.
3. Pour into the glass and serve.

Christmas Sangria

Servings: 5

What you need:

- 1 bottle white wine
- 1 bottle sparkling cider
- 2 oranges, sliced
- 1 red apple, cored and chopped
- 1 green apple, cored and chopped
- 2 cups cranberries

What to do:

1. Combine the wine and cider in a pitcher.
2. Add all of the fruit.
3. Stir well and chill until ready to serve.

cranberry Mimosa

Servings: 5

What you need:

· 1 bottle cranberry juice
· 1 bottle sparkling white wine

What to do:

1. Mix the cranberry juice and sparkling wine together and pour into champagne glasses.
2. Serve!

COLD DRINKS

Salted Caramel Eggnog

Servings: 6

What you need:

- 3 cups whole milk
- 1 cup heavy whipping cream
- 4 cinnamon sticks
- 1 tbsp pure vanilla extract
- 1 tsp grated nutmeg
- 5 eggs
- 2/3 cup sugar
- 1/2 cup caramel syrup
- 1 tbsp sea salt
- 3/4 cup dark rum

What to do:

1. In a large saucepan over medium heat, combine the milk, cream, cinnamon, vanilla, and nutmeg. Bring to a strong simmer. Remove from heat and let sit for 10 minutes.
2. In a large mixing bowl, beat the eggs and sugar on medium high with an electric mixer until fully combined.
3. Pour the egg mixture into the milk and whisk to combine.
4. Add the caramel, sea salt, and rum. Continue whisking.
5. Pour into cups and serve.

  **Consume raw eggs at your own risk.

White Christmas Punch

Servings: 12-16

What you need:

- 1/2 cup sugar
- 1/4 cup hot water
- 3 oz evaporated milk
- 1 tsp almond extract
- 1/2 gallon vanilla ice-cream
- 2 liters of 7-UP
- Whipped cream and Christmas sprinkles, for garnish

What to do:

1. In a glass bowl, stir together the sugar and hot water until the sugar is dissolved.
2. Cool the sugar water and stir in the evaporated milk and almond extract.
3. Pour the mixture into a large punch bowl and add the vanilla ice cream.
4. Use a couple of big spoons or a potato masher to break the ice cream up a bit.
5. Slowly pour in the 7 up.
6. Serve in glasses topped with whipped cream and Christmas sprinkles.

Chocolate Chip Peppermint Milkshake

Servings: 2

What you need:

- 2 cups vanilla ice cream
- 1/2 cup milk
- 1 tsp peppermint extract
- 4 candy canes, crushed
- 1/4 cup chocolate chips
- Whipped cream
- Extra crushed candy canes

What to do:

1. Put the ice cream, milk, peppermint extract, and crushed candy canes in your blender and blend until smooth.
2. Add in the chocolate chips and pulse for a few seconds.
3. Pour into a cup or cups and top with whipped cream and the extra crushed candy canes.

peppermint Milkshake

Servings: 1-2

What you need:

- 3 large scoops of vanilla bean ice cream
- 1/2 tsp peppermint extract
- 3/4 cup milk
- Whipped cream
- 1 candy cane, crushed

What to do:

1. In a blender, blend the ice cream, milk, and peppermint extract.
2. Top with whipped cream and crushed candy canes.

Chocolate peppermint protein Shake

Servings: 1

What you need:

- 1 large banana, frozen
- 2-3 large ice cubes
- 1 cup milk
- 1 scoop chocolate protein powder
- 2 tbsp cocoa powder
- Pinch of sea salt
- 1/4 tsp peppermint extract
- 1 tbsp dark chocolate chips
- Whipped cream

What to do:

1. Place all of the ingredients except the whipped cream in your blender and blend until smooth.
2. Pour into a glass and top with whipped cream.

Eggnog

Servings: 3-4

What you need:

· 6 large egg yolks
· 1/2 cup sugar
· 1 cup heavy cream
· 2 cups milk
· 1 1/2 tsp freshly grated nutmeg
· A pinch of salt
· 1/4 tsp vanilla extract
· 1/8 tsp rum extract

What to do:

1. In a large bowl, whisk together the egg yolks and sugar until creamy.
2. In a large saucepan over medium heat, stir together the heavy cream, milk, nutmeg and salt and bring to a simmer. Stir often.
3. Ladle 1/2 cup of the cream/milk mixture into the egg mixture and whisk vigorously.
4. Ladle in another 1/2 cup of the cream/milk mixture and whisk vigorously. Repeat until all of the cream/milk mixture has been added to the egg mixture.
5. Pour the mixture back into the saucepan over medium heat and continuously whisk until it reaches 160 degrees F on a thermometer.

6. Remove from the heat and stir in the vanilla extract and rum extract.
7. Pour into a pitcher or bowl and refrigerate until chilled.

peppermint Eggnog

Servings: 6-8

What you need:

- 1 quart eggnog
- 3/4 cup white chocolate chips
- 1/3 cup crushed candy canes
- Whipped cream
- Extra crushed candy canes

What to do:

1. In a saucepan over medium heat, combine the eggnog, white chocolate chips, and crushed candy canes in a saucepan. Stir occasionally and heat until the white chocolate is melted.
2. Pour into mugs and top with whipped cream and crushed candy canes.

Grinch Punch

Servings: 16

What you need:

- 1/3 cup sugar
- 1/3 cup water
- 1/3 cup evaporated milk
- 1/2 tsp almond extract
- 12 drops neon green food coloring
- 2 liters lemon lime soda
- 1 pint vanilla ice cream
- 1 pint lime sherbet

What to do:

1. In a large saucepan over medium heat, combine the sugar and water and heat until the sugar is dissolved.
2. Remove the saucepan from the heat and stir in the evaporated milk and almond extract. Cover and refrigerate until chilled.
3. Pour the milk mixture into a large punch bowl. Stir in the food coloring and the lemon-lime soda.
4. Top with the vanilla ice cream and lime sherbet and serve.

HOT DRINKS

Red Velvet Hot Chocolate

Servings: 4

What you need:

- 4 cups whole milk
- 1/4 cup sugar
- 10 oz chocolate chips
- 2 tsp red food coloring
- 1 tsp vanilla extract
- 1/4 cup heavy cream
- 4 oz cream cheese, at room temperature
- 1/2 cup sugar
- 1/2 tsp salt
- 1/2 tsp vanilla extract

What to do:

1. Bring the milk and 1/4 cup sugar to a simmer in a medium saucepan over medium heat. Stir to dissolve the sugar.
2. Remove from heat and stir in the chocolate chips and stir until melted.
3. Stir in the food coloring and vanilla.
4. Pour into serving cups.
5. To make cream cheese topping, whip the whipping cream with an electric mixer until soft peaks form, 5-10 minutes. Set aside.
6. Place the cream cheese, sugar, salt, and vanilla in a separate bowl and mix with electric mixer until combined and creamy.

7. Fold the whipped cream into the cream cheese mixture by hand. Top the hot chocolate with this topping!

cookies and cream Hot chocolate

Servings: 2

What you need:

- 2 cups milk
- 1/2 cup hot chocolate powder
- 1/2 cup Bailey's Irish Cream
- 5 Oreos, finely crushed
- Whipped cream
- Extra crushed Oreos for topping

What to do:

1. Heat the milk in a medium saucepan over medium heat but don't let it boil.
2. When the milk is simmering, add the hot chocolate powder.
3. Add the crushed Oreos to the milk.
4. Remove from the heat and stir in the Bailey's.
5. Serve in a mug topped with whipped cream and crushed Oreos.

Nutella Hot Chocolate

Servings: 4

What you need:

- 4 cups whole milk
- 3 tbsp Nutella
- 2 tbsp unsweetened cocoa powder
- 2 tbsp raw sugar
- Marshmallows, for topping

What to do:

1. Heat the milk in a medium saucepan over medium high heat until simmering.
2. Whisk in the Nutella, cocoa powder, and sugar and mix until dissolved and smooth.
3. Pour into 4 mugs.
4. Top with marshmallows and serve.

peppermint Hot Chocolate

Servings: 4

What you need:

- 2/3 cup heavy whipping cream
- 8 peppermints, crushed
- 4 cups milk
- 8 oz white chocolate, chopped
- 1/2 tsp peppermint extract
- Crushed peppermints, for garnish

What to do:

1. In a medium bowl with a mixer, beat the heavy whipping cream and crushed peppermints until stiff peaks form. Cover and refrigerate.
2. In a large saucepan, heat the milk over medium heat.
3. Add the white chocolate to the milk and whisk until it is melted completely.
4. Stir in the peppermint extract.
5. Ladle the hot chocolate into mugs and top with the whipped cream mixture from the refrigerator.
6. Top the whipped cream with crushed peppermints and serve.

Mint White Hot Chocolate

Servings: 4

What you need:

- 2 cups whole milk
- 2 cups half and half
- 12 oz white chocolate chips
- 1 tsp peppermint extract
- 1/2 tsp vanilla extract
- Green food coloring, optional

What to do:

1. In a large saucepan, add the milk and half and half. Heat over medium until it reaches a light simmer.
2. Stir in the white chocolate chips and stir until melted.
3. Stir in the peppermint and vanilla and food coloring if you're using it.
4. Scoop into cups and serve.

S'mores Hot Chocolate

Servings: 2-3

What you need:

· 3 cups milk
· 1/4 cup cocoa powder
· 2 tbsp chocolate syrup
· 2-3 tbsp sugar
· A pinch of salt
· 1/2 cup Bailey's Irish Cream
· Crushed graham crackers
· 1/2 cup marshmallows

What to do:

1. Preheat your oven to low broil and place a rack in the second to the highest position. Place a baking sheet on the rack.
2. In a saucepan over medium heat, heat the milk until warm but do not boil.
3. When milk is simmering, add the cocoa powder, chocolate syrup, sugar, and salt. Whisk vigorously.
4. Remove from heat and stir in the Bailey's.
5. Pour the hot chocolate into glass mugs.
6. Top the hot chocolate with 1/4 cup of marshmallows each.
7. Carefully place the mugs on the baking sheet in the oven and broil until the marshmallows are browned but not burned! Watch them carefully.

8. Carefully remove the mugs from the oven and sprinkle crushed graham crackers over the marshmallows.

Pumpkin Pie White Hot Chocolate

Servings: 2

What you need:

- 2 cups milk
- 1/2 cup white chocolate chips
- 2 tbsp canned pumpkin
- 1 tbsp corn starch
- 1 tbsp vanilla extract
- Marshmallows

What to do:

1. In a medium saucepan over low heat, add the milk, chocolate chips, pumpkin, corn starch, and vanilla extract.
2. Whisk together until combined and let simmer for 5-7 minutes or until chocolate is melted and liquid is thickened.
3. Pour into two coffee mugs.
4. Top with marshmallows before serving.

Crock Pot Creamy Hot Chocolate

Servings: 8-10

What you need:

- 14-oz can of sweetened condensed milk
- 1 1/2 cups heavy whipping cream
- 6 cups milk
- 1 1/2 tsp vanilla
- 2 cups chocolate chips

What to do:

1. Pour all of the ingredients into your crock pot and stir together well.
2. Cover and cook on low for 2 hours, stirring occasionally.
3. Serve topped with marshmallows.

White Peppermint Hot Chocolate

Servings: 4

What you need:

- 2/3 cup heavy whipping cream
- 8 peppermints, crushed
- 4 cups milk
- 8 oz white chocolate, chopped
- 1/2 tsp peppermint extract
- Crushed peppermints, for garnish

What to do:

1. In a medium bowl with a mixer, beat the heavy whipping cream and crushed peppermints until stiff peaks form. Cover and refrigerate.
2. In a large saucepan, heat the milk over medium heat.
3. Add the white chocolate to the milk and whisk until it is melted completely.
4. Stir in the peppermint extract.
5. Ladle the hot chocolate into mugs and top with the whipped cream mixture from the refrigerator.
6. Top the whipped cream with crushed peppermints and serve.

Crock Pot Apple Cider

Servings: 20+

What you need:

- 2 quarts store bought apple cider
- 1/4 cup brown sugar
- 1/8 tsp ground ginger
- 1 orange, unpeeled and cut into wedges
- 2 cinnamon sticks
- 1 tsp whole cloves
- Cheesecloth

What to do:

1. Tie up the cinnamon sticks and whole clothes in the cheesecloth.
2. Add all of the ingredients to your crock pot.
3. Cover and cook on low for 3 hours.
4. Remove the cheesecloth bag and the orange wedges before serving.
5. Store any leftovers in the refrigerator and reheat before serving.

caramel apple cider

Servings: 12

What you need:

- 12 cups apple juice
- 6 cinnamon sticks
- 1/2 cup caramel sauce
- Whipped cream

What to do:

1. Place the cinnamon sticks and apple juice in your crock pot and cook for 4 hours on high.
2. Stir in the caramel sauce and serve in mugs topped with whipped cream.

caramel Hot chocolate

Servings: 2

What you need:

- 2 cups whole milk
- 1/2 cup chocolate chips
- 1/2 cup caramel sauce
- Marshmallows
- Grated chocolate, as garnish
- Caramel sauce, for drizzling

What to do:

1. In a medium sauce pan over medium heat, add the milk, chocolate chips, and caramel. Whisk until the chocolate chips are melted.
2. Serve warm topped with marshmallows, grated chocolate and caramel sauce.

Crock Pot Mint Hot Chocolate

Servings: 16

What you need:

- 1 gallon of milk
- 20 mini peppermint patties, chopped
- 1 1/2 cups hot chocolate powder
- 1 tbsp vanilla
- Whipped cream
- Chocolate syrup

What to do:

1. Add all of the ingredients to your crock pot, except the whipped cream and chocolate syrup.
2. Heat on low for 2 hours, stirring occasionally.
3. Vigorously beat with a whisk to make the hot chocolate light and frothy.
4. Pour into mugs and top with whipped cream and chocolate syrup.

COFFEE DRINKS

Slow Cooker Gingerbread Latte

Servings: 6-8

What you need:

- 8 cups whole milk
- 1/4 cup maple syrup
- 2 tbsp brown sugar
- 3 tsp ground ginger
- 1 tsp vanilla
- 2 cinnamon sticks
- A pinch of cloves
- 1/2 tsp nutmeg
- 3 1/2 cups strongly brewed coffee or espresso
- Whipped cream and gingerbread man cookies, for garnish

What to do:

1. Add all the ingredients except for the garnishes to your slow cooker and stir.
2. Cook on low for 3 hours, make sure it doesn't boil.
3. Turn the slow cooker to the lowest setting (mine is "keep warm") and cook for another 2 hours.
4. Stir right before serving.
5. Dip into cups and garnish with whipped cream and cookies.

Mocha Peppermint Frappe

Servings: 1-2

What you need:

- 1 1/2 cups strong brewed coffee, partially frozen
- 1/2 cup milk
- 2 tsp unsweetened cocoa powder
- 1 tsp stevia (or to taste)
- 1/2 tsp peppermint extract
- Whipped cream
- Crushed peppermints

What to do:

1. In your blender, combine the coffee, milk, cocoa powder, stevia, and peppermint extract until smooth.
2. Pour into a glass and top with whipped cream and crushed peppermints.

Easy Pumpkin Spice Latte

Servings: 2

What you need:

- 1/2 cup pumpkin puree
- 1 cup French vanilla liquid coffee creamer
- 2 tsp pumpkin pie spice
- 1 1/2 cups hot strong coffee
- Whipped cream
- Cinnamon

What to do:

1. In a medium saucepan over medium heat, whisk together the pumpkin puree, coffee creamer, and pumpkin pie spice until smooth.
2. Reduce the heat to low and simmer for 5 minutes.
3. Pour in the coffee.
4. Pour into coffee mugs and top with whipped cream and cinnamon.
5. Serve immediately.

peppermint Mocha

Servings: 1

What you need:

- 1/4 cup sugar
- 1/4 cup water
- 1/4 tsp peppermint extract
- 3 tbsp powdered cocoa
- 3 tbsp hot water
- 1/2 cup hot espresso or strong brewed coffee
- 1 1/2 cup steamed milk
- Whipped cream

What to do:

1. In a small saucepan over medium heat, stir together the water and sugar. Bring to a boil and let the sugar dissolve. Reduce heat to a simmer and add the peppermint extract. Let simmer for 20 minutes.
2. Mix the cocoa and 3 tbsp of hot water in a mug until a paste forms.
3. Add the espresso and the sugar/water/peppermint mixture to the mug and stir well.
4. Add the milk, stir, and serve.
5. Top with whipped cream.

YOU WILL ALSO ENJOY

WWW.HANNIEPSCOTT.COM/BOOKS

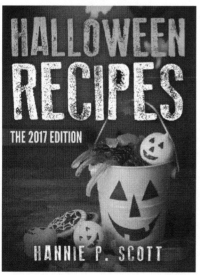

ABOUT THE AUTHOR

Hannie P. Scott, Full-Time Mom and Food Blogger

Driven by her desire for cooking for others (and herself), Hannie spends a lot of time in the kitchen! She enjoys sharing her love of food with the world by creating "no-nonsense" recipe books that anyone can use to make delicious meals.

Hannie attended the University of Southern Mississippi and received a Bachelor's degree in Nutrition & Dietetics. She enjoys cooking and experimenting with food. She hopes to inspire readers and help them build confidence in their cooking. All Hannie's recipes are easy-to-prepare with easy-to-acquire ingredients.

For more recipes, cooking tips, and Hannie's blog, visit:

www.HanniePScott.com

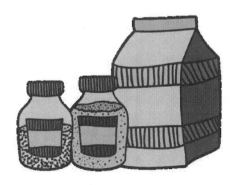

NOTES

NOTES

NOTES

NOTES

NOTES

NOTES

Manufactured by Amazon.ca
Bolton, ON

16189411R00039